WHAT'S IN THE BOTTLE?

DARLENE JOHNSON CARGILL

PAGE PUBLISHING, INC.
Conneaut Lake, PA

First originally published by Page Publishing 2021

ISBN 978-1-6624-0169-5 (pbk)
ISBN 978-1-6624-0170-1 (digital)

Printed in the United States of America

I'm grateful to my son Kenneth Johnson, Jr., for his encouragement to "write your book" as well as my bonus children Jessica and Corey Cargill. And, a special thank you to my "young editor" Jordyn Wynne for her input and suggestions.

Kendra was an only child. Her mother chose the name Kendra because it meant "wisdom" and she wanted her daughter to be wise.

She lived in a two-bedroom apartment with her mom. She did not believe she had many friends because she was quiet and shy. If anyone asked, she would say her mom was her best friend.

When not at school, she kept to herself most of the time, in her bedroom, which was pink and purple, her favorite colors.

Kendra loved talking to her mom in the evenings when she came home from work.

Most evenings, she would sit at the kitchen counter doing her homework while her mom prepared dinner.

These were her favorite times because she could talk to her mom, uninterrupted.

One particular evening, while her mom was beginning to prepare dinner, Kendra sat at the kitchen counter and looked up from doing her homework and started a conversation with her mom.

"Mom?" she called out.

"Yes, dear?" her mom answered.

"I'm feeling some kind of way, but I don't know how to describe it."

Her mom looked surprised and said, "Tell me more."

Kendra searched for the right words.

"Sometimes I feel like a bottle with a cork on top. The cork keeps everything inside the bottle, and I want to take the cork out and pour out everything, but I'm afraid, and I don't know what to do. What should I do, Mom?"

Her mom looked up from cutting carrots and said, "Hmmm?"

"Sweetie, I think you have to have a strategy to empty out the bottle a little bit at a time, and eventually, you will get to the bottom of the bottle. What's inside of the bottle now?" Kendra's mom wanted to know.

Kendra answered, "A lot of things, mostly my feelings. I know when I'm feeling sad, but there are times I'm not sure how I feel."

"Okay," her mom said. "I know we don't always talk about our feelings, but how you feel is very important. Just remember," her mom paused then said, "when it comes to identifying what or how you're feeling, having a strategy is very important.

"First, you have to think about how you're feeling. Are you feeling sad, happy, excited, or scared? Then you have to take the cork out of your bottle and pour out a little of your feelings that are inside.

"When I'm not sure how I feel, my strategy is to write down my thoughts, and that helps me to identify my feelings," said her mom. "Your strategy may be different from mine, and that's okay," she added.

"Okay, thanks, Mom," Kendra said, and she went back to doing her homework.

The very next day, when her mom came home from work, she handed Kendra a beautifully wrapped box.

Kendra was very excited and surprised because her birthday was months away.

"For me!" she said with excitement, as she quickly and carefully began to unwrap the box. She didn't want to rip the pink and purple wrapping paper.

Inside the box was a decorated purple bottle with a pink cork on top. "Oh, Mom," Kendra said, "I love it!"

Kendra took the bottle to her room and placed it on the table beside her bed.

She began to think of a strategy she would use to empty out her feelings. She was going to pretend that all her feelings were inside the bottle.

The next morning, looking at the bottle, she thought about what her mom had said about feelings and a strategy.

Feelings are very important. You have to first think about how you're feeling and then pour out a little bit at a time.

Holding her bottle, she thought to herself, *My bottle feels heavy*.

Kendra said aloud, "When I feel afraid, I should take the cork out and pretend to pour out some of my feelings."

The next morning, while getting ready for school, Kendra felt a stirring in her stomach.

She picked up her purple bottle and said, "I feel afraid that nobody will like me, and I have no friends at school."

While clutching her bottle, Kendra took a deep breath and took the cork out of the bottle, turned it upside down, shook it, and quickly put the cork back in.

She took another deep breath and said to herself, "That wasn't so hard." She smiled and placed the bottle back on her bedside table and headed off to school.

During the school day, there was a moment when Kendra struggled with a math problem. She whispered to herself, "I'm feeling annoyed." She then stopped and immediately thought of her bottle at home. And she took a deep breath and went on with her schoolwork.

The next time, a few days later, when she picked up her bottle, it felt much lighter.

She stared at her bottle and smiled. Then she took the cork out once again.

Kendra turned the bottle upside down, shook it gently, and said, "I'm feeling sad. I want to play and run at recess with the other kids, but I'm afraid I can't run fast. And I don't have a best friend to play with at school."

She put the cork back in.

Each day for weeks, she uncorked her bottle, turned it upside down, and poured out new feelings.

"I'm feeling anxious because I don't know what to wear to school. I'm feeling unattractive because my hair is too straight, and I wish it was curlier. I wish I was pretty like my mom. I'm nervous because I have a math test. I'm sad because my teacher didn't call on me in class. I'm scared something may happen to my mom."

Kendra voiced many of her feelings. She then let out a big sigh and got dressed for school.

Then after weeks of pouring out the contents in her bottle, she picked up the bottle and thought to herself, *My bottle feels so much lighter.*

And she no longer felt anxious, sad, scarred, worried, or afraid. She felt happier.

She took the cork out of the bottle and looked inside.

"It's really empty," she said. She had a big smile on her face and placed the bottle on the shelf. This time, she did not put the cork back in.

She couldn't wait to tell her mom how happy she felt and to thank her again for the gift of the beautiful purple bottle with a pink cork on top.

Kendra ran to her mom's bedroom and saw something she had not noticed before. On her mom's bedside table, next to her journal, was a pink bottle with a red cork in it.

About the Author

Darlene Johnson Cargill is passionate about children's issues and writes stories to help them navigate the landscape of their life. She has worked as a reporter for a daily newspaper and a freelance writer for local and national publications. Following her retirement from a large corporation, she began working as a substitute in the Orange City School District in Ohio. This is her first children's book.

CPSIA information can be obtained
at www.ICGtesting.com
Printed in the USA
BVHW010843090323
660077BV00019B/339